MW00881372

GOD

and

SCIENCE

A Road Map to Miracles Using PSYCH-K®

LINDA GAUTHIER

BALBOA.PRESS
A DIVISION OF HAY HOUSE

Balboa Press books may be ordered through booksellers or by contacting:

Balboa Press
A Division of Hay House
1663 Liberty Drive
Bloomington, IN 47403
www.balboapress.com
844-682-1282

Because of the dynamic nature of the Internet, any web addresses or links contained in this book may have changed since publication and may no longer be valid. The views expressed in this work are solely those of the author and do not necessarily reflect the views of the publisher, and the publisher hereby disclaims any responsibility for them.

The author of this book does not dispense medical advice or prescribe the use of any technique as a form of treatment for physical, emotional, or medical problems without the advice of a physician, either directly or indirectly. The intent of the author is only to offer information of a general nature to help you in your quest for emotional and spiritual well-being. In the event you use any of the information in this book for yourself, which is your constitutional right, the author and the publisher assume no responsibility for your actions.

Print information available on the last page.

ISBN: 978-1-9822-5510-7 (sc)
ISBN: 978-1-9822-5511-4 (hc)
ISBN: 978-1-9822-5512-1 (e)

Library of Congress Control Number: 2020918006

Balboa Press rev. date: 10/01/2020

This book is dedicated to:

My two sisters, Patricia and Kathy, who have always been there for me and supported me.

My two daughters, Angela and Kristine, who are amazing women in the world. They taught me more than I could ever teach them.

My grandchildren, Skylar, Mason, and Camille, who have kept me young, except when I was teaching them to drive.

My grandchildren, Rachael, Alec, and Isaac, who inspire me every day as they lovingly and courageously, create a kinder world.

The love of my life, Bob, who changed the trajectory of my life.

PREFACE

Science has caught up with spirituality, and they are working in tandem.

There is a power that exists in the world that you can use. This power can be demonstrated by quantum science and by Spirit. You have always been using this power. Most of us have been unaware of this power and have been operating on auto pilot. We use this cosmic energy to support our fears and limiting beliefs. We must first become aware of what these fears and limiting beliefs are. Then, by using the new brain science, we can replace them with beliefs of health, wealth, peace, and fulfillment. It is your beliefs, not your genes, that are creating your life. This book is an instruction manual that will show you how to access and use this invisible cosmic power to create miracles.

You've been given this amazing gift of life. Much can be accomplished in the duration of a lifetime. Quantum physics demonstrates that your energy ripples out into the world. You are impacting everything around you. You can raise your vibration and raise the energy level of the entire universe.

What we think and what we believe is controlling our life. Your power to change is in your subconscious mind. I will introduce you to a process that allows you to make changes in your beliefs and thus make real, sustainable changes in your life. My vision is that by reading this book, your vibration will be lifted, and by applying these processes, your life will be changed dramatically, as I have seen happen for so many others.

In this book, I use the name *God*. This creative force in the universe goes by many names: Jehovah, Yahweh, Divine, Vishnu, Allah, Spirit, First Cause, Most High, Krishna, Mother Nature, or Ralph. We each have our own understanding and interpretation of God. It is personal.

Please know that this book is for people of all faiths or of none.

If you want to awaken all of humanity, then awaken yourself

If you want to eliminate the suffering in the world, then eliminate all that is dark and negative in yourself

The greatest gift you have to give is that of your own self transformation

LAU TZU

CONTENTS

ACKNOWLEDGMENTS

I want to thank Rocky Costello, who opened me up to knowing that all things are possible.

I want to thank Karen McKy, the best teacher I have ever had. She is a dear friend who keeps me out of trouble.

I am grateful to my dear friend Selena Sage, my warrior protector, teacher, and confidant.

INTRODUCTION

Here is proof that on a spiritual level and a scientific level there is a cosmic power that we are always using. Most of us use it unconsciously and do not even recognize that it is available to us.

We are operating on autopilot and reacting to every circumstance that shows up in our lives. We misuse this power and continue to support our fears and limiting beliefs. Our lives are stuck and will not change. We keep repeating the same painful and destructive patterns.

This power is mysterious and baffling and very exciting when we learn how to harness and focus it for our own creations. You can call it quantum science, or you can call it God or just cosmic energy. Awaken yourself to the possibilities of a new life. What would you like? Health? Wealth? Loving relationships? Learn about this power and how to use it.

I learned about consciousness and that the mind is the tool that we can use for change. I used affirmations and positive thinking. Why wasn't this working? What I learned was that I was using the wrong part of my mind. I found the new brain science and here at last was the key that opened the hidden part of my mind and allowed me to make changes. I tested it out and experienced my own transformation, and then I watched as others changed after using this same process.

For most of my life, I did not know that I had the ability to paint, and then I became an artist. I found a process that simplified the art of painting. I was excited about the method and successfully shared it with others. To my joy, I was able to facilitate others to open themselves to their creativity, and my students became accomplished artists.

Just as I had found a replicable way that people could learn how to paint a gallery-quality picture their first time at the easel, I had found a replicable way people could tap into their power to create the life that they have always wanted. In both cases, I was able to find a way to take something that is considered complicated and difficult and show a path that is clear, easy to understand, and easy to put into action. I am inspired to share this path with you. You can live in joy, love, and beauty as you are meant to. You can raise your vibration, and you can raise the vibration of the universe. You are powerful, and your energy ripples out to everything.

My vision is that by reading this book, your vibration will be lifted, and by applying these processes, your life will be changed dramatically, as I have seen happen for so many others.

CHAPTER 1

THE NEW FRONTIER

We are spiritual beings and we are born into a physical world. Our early years are about learning how to function on the physical plane; how to walk, feed ourselves, support our body functions and provide material things that make us comfortable. At this level we will accept anything that comes into our life as "this is life and there is nothing I can do about it." We perceive things to be coincidence, luck and unconnected.

With experience we discover cause and effect and make connections. As we observe nature and study world religions we begin to get a glimpse of a world beyond the physical. Spiritual leaders have been telling us for centuries about the power of God that presides over the Universe. Until now we have had no tangible proof of how this power works. With advanced technology we can measure subtle energies and with computers we can compile and analyize vast amounts of data. Now we are able to understand this electromagnetic power from the viewpoint of hard science. We are seeing that spiritual laws are the same laws that are governing quantum science.

What we are discovering is that this force, this energy is in us and is working in our lives everyday. Our mind is always creating with this energy whether on purpose or by default. Here is a roadmap that will show you how you can use this energy to manifest the life of your dreams.

Miracles are at your fingertips. You may have been told that "everything you need to know is inside of you." How do you access this inner sanctum where all your wisdom resides? This book is about finding the source of your power and how to focus it to create miracles.

We are entering a new frontier. With technology and quantum science, we have the ability to analyze mass data and measure subtle energy. We are able to see our lives and the universe from a new perspective. From this new perspective, we see connections we never suspected were there. We begin to see a power that operates throughout the universe. We can harness this power and use it to make our lives more fulfilling and the planet a better place to live.

What I'm going to share with you is information that has transformed thousands of people's lives. It completely changed my life and the lives of everyone I have introduced it to. It has saved marriages, increased money, created health, helped people find their perfect mate, broken the habit of smoking, supported addicts to stay clean, created sustained weight loss, reduced anxiety, and brought peace of mind. What is contained in this book is a remembrance of something of that you have always known but do not know that you know. You will find a tool that allows you to access this knowledge. My hope is that this work will undo every source of pain, suffering, and failure and assist in the evolution of human consciousness in each of us and raise us to the level of peace and joy that we are meant to have.

Science has caught up with spirituality. Spiritual law is now being objectively proved in laboratories. On a quantum level, spiritual powers are backed up by scientific evidence.

The key to changing your life is in your subconscious mind. You can access the part of your mind that is below your consciousness. Using the new brain science, you are able to find the negative messages, fears, beliefs, and past traumas that are creating poor choices and bad outcomes in your life. You will be empowered to replace these with life-affirming beliefs that will create health, wealth, and joy. You can make changes in behaviors and habits easily and effortlessly that will change your life, without years of talk therapy. There are immediate and sustainable changes. *This is amazing! This is exciting! This is life-changing!*

Take a good look at your life. What would you like to change? You may have success in some areas of your life, but you may be blocked in other areas. Until recently, you could only know what was going on in your subconscious mind by the results that were showing up in your life. The people, places, conditions, and things in your life are the effects of the beliefs in your subconscious mind. Whatever you believe about yourself, you will go out into the world and look for or create situations that validate your beliefs. If you have low self-esteem, you will cower and set low levels of aspiration for yourself. If you see yourself as powerful, you will be confident and reach your full potential.

You can change the results that are showing up in your life by changing your beliefs.

You have been using your willpower and positive thinking to make these changes. How's that working for you? There is an easier, faster, and more direct way. We start with what you want to change. Would you like more money? Better health? Loving relationships? You will determine what you would like to have in your life. This is what we will focus on. This is your starting point. Being unique individuals, we each have our own desires and priorities. Your life, you choose. When you decide what you want, together we can get more clarity around it if you need it. We can then make the changes.

CHAPTER 2

MY STORY

I was sent on my spiritual journey at a very early age. My mother died when I was four years old, and my alcoholic father abandoned us. My paternal grandparents took me and my two sisters in. Every Sunday we were dropped off at the Nazarene church for Sunday school. This is an evangelical church that believes that there is a real heaven and hell in the afterlife. We are born sinners, and we must repent and be saved in this lifetime or to hell we go. If you are redeemed, you can always sin and get sent back to hell. I was unclear about the rules and what I needed to do to get out of hell. I knew that there was a harsh, judgmental God in the sky.

My grandfather was a Southern Baptist, and my grandmother was a Christian Scientist. One of my grandmother's sisters was instrumental in building the Nazarene church in Santa Monica, and I think Grandma and Grandpa dropped us off there on Sundays so they could get a break. Neither of them promoted the teaching.

When I was ten, my grandma refused medical treatment for breast cancer because of her religion. She died, and Grandpa was not equipped to raise us. We never went back to the Nazarene church.

When my mother was dying, she asked her best friend, Louise, to take care of us. This wonderful lady, who was in the middle of a divorce at the time grandma died honored her promise to our mother and took us in. Shortly after coming to live with

Louise her daughter, Beth (our adopted sister) died. She was born with cerebral palsy and had a weak heart. She died at the age of sixteen.

Louise was agnostic, and she married Irving, who was Jewish.

Because of all the death I had experienced, I was always trying to figure out why we were here. People came, and they disappeared. What does it all mean? I started reading whatever metaphysical books I could find. I read philosophy and psychology and studied world religions. I read a book called *Your Mind Can Make You Sick or Well.* I was fascinated and wanted to know more.

When I was in my teens, I decided to give religion another try. I began visiting churches of different denominations. I had been raised by a Catholic, a Southern Baptist, a Christian Scientist, an Agnostic, and a Jew. Each church I attended told me that their belief was the only way to a good life and salvation. I knew this was wrong. The people who were raising me were of many faiths, and they were all good people. This message, when taken to the extreme, is "You must believe as I do, or I must kill you." To me, violence is not God's will. And there was dogma. You need to believe and live by these rules on blind faith. In the Nazarene church, there were rules against wearing makeup and dancing. The Catholic Church was constantly changing their rules. You can't eat meat on Friday, and you can't get a divorce. Then the rules changed. You *can* eat meat on Friday, and you can get an annulment if everyone signs the right papers and you give the church enough money. For breaking some rules, there was punishment of excommunication or shunning. Where is that Christian forgiveness? I remember putting money in an envelope at one church that I attended and then putting the envelope in the offering basket. The envelope had spaces for me to write my name and address, and I filled it out. That church began sending me notices telling me that I was expected to keep sending money. If this was religion, I didn't want anything to do with it.

My saving grace was that as I studied world religions, I discovered the common thread that continued through all of them. I realized that these were principles that resonated with me: kindness, compassion, truth, love, and integrity. Although religion wasn't discussed in my home, these principles were practiced. It was a serious offense if I didn't return a library book on time.

I had a spiritual awakening when I was in my thirties. I was on the brink of leaving my marriage. I felt I had failed. I took my vows seriously, and I had two daughters and knew this would cause them great pain. I had married a man who had a temper and very different values and morals than I had. I tried for twelve years to see if the marriage could get better, and it didn't. This was a low point in my life.

I had survived my childhood and had come out of it with low self-esteem. My childhood had been traumatic and unstable.

I had three sets of parents, each with different expectations. I had a right to feel sorry for myself, didn't I?

As I walked by the water's edge in Malibu, I began to get a very different perspective on everything. I saw the beauty and perfection of the tapestry of my life. I saw how God had protected me, and I became aware of the love I had been given. I had been exposed to truths and lessons and different ways to be in the world. I learned to trust: "Leap and the net will appear." As we lost each set of parents, another came for us. Each experience was necessary and prepared us for our next. The loving people who had taken us in had sacrificed for us. It is not a small thing to take in three girls. The mistakes I had made were really interesting experiences and stepping-stones to success. From that moment, I could no longer be a victim. In fact, I felt like I had been given a crash course in spirituality. From this perspective, I could feel God's grace. What amazing gifts this childhood had given me!

I've gotten other messages. Bob, my second husband, and I were traveling through France. We saw beautiful art work in the Paris museums. Then we went to the places that were the subjects of the artists' work: the cathedral at Rouen that Monet painted thirty times, his home in Giverny, the garden, the town of Auvers-sur-Oise where Van Gogh lived, the café, the fields, and the church he painted. As we visited each location, I kept getting a message. In my mind, the message "You can do this" kept repeating. It wasn't a voice but a message that came through clearly. When I returned home, I began to look for an art teacher or school. After a year of searching and trying different media, I found a man, Dominic Vignola, who taught a tonal way of laying out the palette and then painting on canvas, without any drawing. I was able to get gallery-quality oil-on-canvas paintings in no time. I had always loved art. I found my History of Art class in college fascinating. But I had no idea that I could paint. And there it was—I was an artist!

The path of an artist has brought me many wonderful experiences. I have taught this method of painting and opened many people up to their creativity. My students have produced wonderful paintings and have become accomplished artists. It was very fulfilling to watch this unfold. I was invited to France to teach. I have been commissioned by celebrities to do their portraits.

I pay attention so I don't miss the messages. They often begin as a whisper, and if I don't pay attention, they become a scream. I've learned that they are important.

It was late in life that I discovered a church that resonated with all I believed: the Center for Spiritual Living. All the books I had been reading were in their bookstore. The message from the minister was positive and inspiring. All religions are of value, and there are many paths to God. In this teaching, I wasn't asked to follow their rules on blind faith. I was asked to try their spiritual principles and see how they worked for me. There was no dogma. Here I found community. I had never been part of a spiritual community before. The exchange of ideas, the love and support have added to my spiritual growth.

CHAPTER 3

GOD

When I refer to God I am talking about First Cause of Everything, Giver of Life, Ruler of the Universe and Source of All Moral Authority, Surpreme Being, and Holy Spirit. God's power comes to us through our mind.

How do we see God? There came a day when I asked God to reveal Himself to me. So this day as I often do, I put on my rollerblades and bladed down the bike path that runs along the beach. There is a 3-foot tall cinder block wall that separates the bike path from the sand. After skating awhile I began to see words that were written in chalk on the wall. These words were about 2 feet tall and were smudged with age but were easy to read. They were very spiritual words: Forgiveness, kindness, blessed, love, transformation, freedom, enlightenment, peace, the words kept coming. They went on for blocks. The words had been there awhile, but I had never seen them before and I had skated past them many times. Then I skated past a home I saw every time I skated and I always took a good look at it because the architecture was interesting and the landscaping was beautiful. This day I saw something I had never seen before. There in the front yard was a peace pole. It was a 6 sided pole with words "May peace prevail on earth" written on it in many languages.

God had revealed Himself to me. And the message I received was, "I am now and always will be here for you. You just need to look." And with that confirmation my heart was singing.

Now I see God everywhere: the beating of my heart, the endless crashing of the waves in the ocean, the sunrise and the sunset, the flowers and the trees, the hummingbird visiting me on my patio and the dolphin playing in the waves.

How do we hear God? His messages come through thoughts, ideas, inspiration, intuition, and meditation. We may hear something or even overhear something. Messages may come from something we've read, seen in a movie, a dream, or even a road sign.

God speaks to you through thoughts and feelings. His message brings feelings of peace. What He is telling you will resonate with you and you will recognize Truth.

Messages from God may repeat themselves. When something comes to me 3 times I know that God is speaking to me. These messages come to me in the most random ways. Just as we each have our own connection to our God we each have our own method of receiving His messages. Think about it. How do messages come to you?

God connects with us through our consciousness. One of the most exciting new frontiers in the last century is the discovery of consciousness. Our mind has the power to shape our lives and our planet. With this knowledge and the new brain science, all things are possible. Pain and stress dissolve, and lives are transformed. We are living in a time when we can accelerate our human potential beyond anything we have ever imagined.

We are all spiritual beings having a human experience. Each one of us is valuable. We have come here for a purpose. This is a purposeful universe. Everything in the universe is connected to everything else. The achievement of every individual contributes to the advancement and well-being of the whole. When we feel separated from each other and the divine, we lose sight of our purpose. The source of all our difficulties and challenges in life comes down to the belief in separation from divinity—the divinity of each of us, the divinity of all humankind, and the divinity of our environment. When we get beyond the illusion of separation, the reality of wholeness becomes clear: wholeness in body, mind, and spirit.

There are core spiritual principles held to be true across cultures: love is more powerful than hate; truth sets us free; forgiveness liberates both sides; unconditional love heals; courage empowers; and the essence of divinity is peace.

There are core truths of the world's great spiritual traditions: kindness and compassion to everything and everyone (including oneself), humility, forgiveness, simplicity, loving as a way of being, reverence for all of life, devotion to truth, and surrender to God.

These sacred truths were embraced by our great spiritual leaders. Religions were formed: Christianity, Buddhism, Hinduism, Islam, and Judaism. When we go to the pure teachings and study how these spiritual leaders lived, we discover the embodiment of God.

When the Dalia Lama was asked what his religion is, he answered, "My religion is kindness."

The downfall of all lofty spiritual teachings has been their misinterpretations by the less enlightened and by the challenges of inaccurate translations. Scripture can be quoted to justify any position. Spiritual teachings remain hearsay and are therefore prone to distortion and misunderstanding. The "righteous" are always dangerous because of their unbalanced perception, their harsh judgement and their indifference to moral violence.

In this interconnected universe, every improvement we make in our private world improves the world at large for everyone. It is a scientific fact that "what is good for you is good for me." Simple kindness to oneself and all that lives is the most powerful transformational force of all. We are hardwired to feel warm inside when we are doing a kind deed. It increases one's true power. It can't be practiced with the expectation of some selfish gain or reward. In a universe where like goes to like, we attract what we emanate.

Consequences may come in an unsuspected way. For instance, you help an elderly lady carry her groceries to the car, and a week later, a helpful stranger gives you a hand when you have lost your keys. You are aware that you have done a good deed, but you probably will not connect it to the kind deed that is done for you one week later. The synchronicity of the events may go unnoticed. An observable *this* does not cause an observable *that*. What is happening, in reality, is that you have made a shift in motive, intent, and behavior. It acts on a field that produces an increased likelihood of positive responses.

Our kindnesses are like building up a bank account of good deeds, but one from which we cannot draw on our own personal will. The way the funds are distributed is that there is a catalyst released before this reciprocal kindness will show up in our lives. This leads us to believe that "God works in mysterious ways" because we often can't make this connection.

Your subconscious mind is fertile and literal. The thoughts you are thinking are the realities you are bringing into your life.

"If you think you can do a thing or if you think you can't do a thing, either way you are right."—Henry Ford

Henry Ford was a visionary. He launched the car culture in America. He perfected the combustion engine. In 1913, he installed the assembly line in his Model T Ford factory. This brought the time to build a car from twelve hours to two hours and thirty minutes, and the cost of the car dropped from seven thousand dollars to three hundred sixty dollars. Even though workers' hours were cut, he didn't cut their wages. Instead, he nearly doubled their pay to five dollars a day. This was a gamble that paid off. The wage increase enabled his workers to purchase the cars they were producing.

It is our mind through which God makes contact and when we have faith in our ability to create our dreams we can change the world.

CHAPTER 4

SCIENCE

Newtonian science was predictable and constant. When an experiment was duplicated, the results were always the same. We were working with things in the physical world—beakers, elements, heat, cold, liquids, and solids; things we could see, touch, and feel. I struggled through high school chemistry and had to copy others' laboratory results. Somehow my experiments just didn't work out—and that was basic stuff. We now have something that is much more complicated.

No one was ready to accept quantum science when it was discovered. This made everyone uncomfortable. A structured scientific mind yearned to stay with Newtonian science where, on a physical level, everything was simple and predictable. Quantum physics is considered to be complex and incredibly difficult. Discovered in the 1920s, scientists tried to dismiss it. There was no consistency. How could they work without dependability and consistency?

Now, don't panic, because I'm going to talk about quantum physics. I will be explaining it on the comprehension level of a five-year-old, because that is the level that I can understand it on. Remember how much trouble I had with chemistry? You see, no one understands quantum physics. It's like electricity; we don't know how it works, but we know enough about its properties to be able to harness it for our use. So we'll be talking about the mysterious ways quantum physics works.

You don't need to understand quantum science. I just want you to be amazed and know that at this level all things are possible. It will make as much sense as a dolphin playing piano. Even sophisticated physicists call this phenomenon "weird and spooky." I know I said I would simplify quantum physics; I didn't say I would make it logical. So disconnect your logical brain and just be entertained by the crazy way this stuff works.

We are talking about the smallest things in our universe and the fundamental rules of the universe.

Quantum physics seems outside us, but it is happening in our bodies continuously.

Subatomic particles move as both particles and waves. So, think of tiny little baseballs being thrown, and then think of the way water moves in a wave motion. A subatomic particle can move using either method of travel.

According to Heisenberg's Uncertainty Theory, we can measure either the location of the particle or its momentum, but not both at the same time. The same is true for the energy and the place in time of the particle. Just the act of measuring one changes the value of the other. Consequently, in quantum mechanics, we can only estimate the probability of any result.

A subatomic particle can be found in two places at the same time. What? Nonlinear dynamics emerged. This is the concept that life is like a hologram, and everything is happening at the same time; you know, time travel. This may be difficult to wrap your head around, so don't even try. Just know that on this level, time is irrelevant.

Subatomic particles can entangle. Imagine two coins that are magically entangled. It's as if they share the same history and have a cosmic connection. I take one coin, and you take the other. We toss our coins. Mine lands heads up, and yours lands tails up. Mine will always spin heads up, and yours will always spin tails up.

The entanglement has mysteriously linked the two coins. When I can manipulate my coin and get it to spin tails up, your coin will change its spin to heads up. The coins will always spin in the opposite direction. As an observer, we may conclude that the change is happening sequentially, but your coin is actually changing at the exact same time mine is changing. They behave as though they send signals instantaneously to each other, and this connection will hold, no matter how far apart they are. You can send your coin out to the space station, and our coins will still be entangled. This is how subatomic particles work. Einstein called this "spooky action at a distance. With the discoveries of Einstein, Heisenberg, Bell, Bohr, and others, our model of the universe expanded rapidly. Advanced theoretical physics demonstrated that everything in the universe is subtly dependent upon and interactive with everything else.

Chaos means a mass of apparently meaningless data, for instance, a bunch of dots. Looking at the dots, one can't see any organized pattern. There are unsuspected connections, and yet these dots seem unrelated and random. With the advent of advanced computer technology, patterns emerged. It was discovered that what appears to be incoherent actually has an inner hidden coherence. Now we are able to make sense of apparently random natural phenomena. With the abrupt access to formerly inconceivable masses of data, we are able to get a larger perspective on the chaos theory. We discovered that what appeared to be chaos was really only a limited perception. When we can see the larger picture, it all begins to make sense. An important element of the chaos theory is the law of "sensitive dependence on initial conditions." I know, I got a little technical there. All this refers to is the fact that a slight variation over a course of time can change the trajectory and produce a profoundly different outcome. We know that a ship whose course is one degree off will find itself hundreds of miles from its intended destination.

On a subatomic level it is clear that everything is energy.

At this level the results of any given experiment can't be predicted. It can only be forecast in terms of probabilities. The scientist, when running two duplicate experiments, will get one result when the experiment is being observed and a different result when the experiment is not being observed. This demonstrates that even our presence influences things around us. You enter a room, and the atmosphere is changed.

Ask a physicist what exactly is a subatomic particle and their answer will be, "I don't know if anyone can give you an answer." Scientists work with the rules of quantum theory without knowing why particles act so strangely at the smallest level.

When engineers build devices, they do so by following rules that they don't fully understand. Quantum theory is like a recipe. If you have all the ingredients and follow the steps, you end up with a meatloaf. But using quantum theory to build technology is like following a recipe without knowing how or why the meat, eggs, and breadcrumbs (subatomic particles) are becoming a meatloaf. Sure, you can put together a good meatloaf, but you can't explain what happens to the ingredients during the process. Please don't follow this recipe to make meatloaf. You'll be sorry.

Everything is energy, and as energy, everything is fluid and ever changing. Energy cannot be contained. It influences the field around it, and as it turns out, it goes out into the world and influences the universe. We have been catapulted into the age of technology. Has anyone noticed how fast this is all going? MRIs, computer chips, nuclear power plants, cell phones, space travel.

For a time, we tried to ignore the invisible quantum field of Einstein, in which matter is actually made up of energy and there are no absolutes. At the atomic level, matter does not even exist with certainties; it exists as a tendency to exist. What? Is this crazy enough for you? All rules about biology and physics are shattered.

The concept of matter is an illusion; everything in the universe is made up of energy. Living organisms refuse to be quantified. There are healings that allopathic medicine can't explain. What about tumor suppression, spontaneous healings, psychic phenomena, amazing feats of strength and endurance, acupuncturists' ability to relieve pain by moving chi around in the body, and the ability to walk on hot coals without getting burned?

Every material structure in the universe, including you and me, radiates a unique signature. Thousands of years ago, long before Western scientists discovered quantum physics, Asians honored energy as the principal factor contributing to health and well-being. Medical quantum research has been in hundreds and hundreds of scientific studies over the last fifty years. They have consistently revealed that "invisible forces" of the electromagnetic spectrum profoundly impact every facet of biology. The research has been published in respected medical journals. It is only in the last 2 years that medical schools have started to include information about the mind/

body connection. Doctors are still predominantly being trained to use Newtonian science. Do the pharmaceutical companies have anything to do with the withholding of this very valuable information? After all, it is the pharmaceutical companies that fund the medical schools.

Cosmic energy is something that can't be patented or sold.

CREATING YOUR DREAMS

So, if our minds can move energy and everything is energy, why haven't we created the life of our dreams? The life we desire must begin with the creation process. We must get the idea of what we want. Write down the things you would like to have in your life and imagine them in detail. These are your hopes and dreams. This will be your to-do list. You can create a video of your vision board by going to mindmovies.com. There is a template that you can use to make a movie of what you want in your life.

To-Do List

- Satisfying job that creates a lot of money
- Comfortable home
- New car
- Vibrant health
- Loving relationships

These are general examples, and your list will be more detailed and personal to you. The vision of how you will feel when you have attained these goals will motivate you to keep moving in that direction.

Ester Hicks, author and lecturer, calls them "Rockets of Desire." All of nature exhibits abundance: sand on the beach, fish in the ocean, planets in the galaxy. God demonstrates abundance, and He wants you to live in abundance. Every person wants to be all that they can be. We need basic things in order to live fully in body: good food, comfortable clothing, warm shelter, and leisure time.

To live fully in mind I need books and time to study them, I need time to travel and observe, I need intellectual companionship and money to help others who are less fortunate. The desire for riches is really the desire for a richer, more abundant life. Being rich is a worthy goal to put on your to-do list.

"There is no passion to be found in playing small—in settling for a life that is less than the one you are capable of living."—Nelson Mandela

When you have achieved one of your goals, take time to celebrate your accomplishment. You may get great pleasure, and you gain confidence in your ability to create. Sometimes you may be surprised that achieving a goal doesn't give you the joy you expected.

Material comforts may be a starting point on one's journey in life, but you begin to realize that it is not your final destination. There is another list. This is one that we generally forget to put on our vision board.

This is our master list; one that is always motivating us, even as we are chasing our to-do list. This is the to-be list.

To-Be List

- Living in harmony with nature
- Knowing the universe is a safe place
- Living in love, not fear
- Choosing compassion and forgiveness
- Allowing creativity to flow
- Seeing everyone as one and all connected

Striving for the principles on this list leads you to peace, serenity, and joy. We are human BEings, not human DOings. So allow yourself to be. This is about getting out of the bussyness of chasing after the stuff and things that are on your to-do list and begin work on your to-be list. The reality is that the things on this list are not goals but principles. These are not items to be checked off the list. This is a list of your state of being and something that you will always be living. We believe that getting that high-paying, fulfilling job will bring us security and peace. But that's backward. When we have achieved security and peace inside ourselves, the high-paying, fulfilling job will be attracted to us.

Be aware that your to-do list is temporary and ever changing. You will check things off as they are completed, scratch them off as you decide you no longer want them, and you are always adding to the list.

What's on the to-do list isn't important. When you have achieved one goal, another "Rocket of Desire" will show up. The important part of this list is that it is the catalyst that motivates you to start your journey.

It is all about the journey and who you are on the journey.

Are you living the principles that are on your to-be list? This list is permanent, unchanging, and important. Truly, as you become more practiced with the to-be list, all else is accomplished for you. You live in the magic of serendipity. All the right people, opportunities, creative ideas, and inspiration will come to you. All you will need will show up, and you will be guided to the next step. You are in the flow. The collateral effects are that you will be checking items off your to-do list; they will just come.

It is as if you are living in a state of grace as you watch your dreams manifest before you. Yes, there may be what feels like boulders blocking you on your journey. Keep operating on the principles that are on your to-be list and be surprised at the new opportunities that show up for you.

HEALING

The mind has a powerful influence on the body and helps the body heal.

You see, when you consider the body on a quantum science level, anything is possible. Diseases considered terminal are healed. Conditions that are considered hopeless disappear. We have the ability to take cosmic energy into our bodies and create health. Using energy frequencies is the medicine of the future. Do you believe that your body can heal itself, or do you need a doctor and a medical procedure? We have been trained to believe that Western medicine has all our answers.

Western doctors have learned how to apply the placebo effect. The placebo or sugar pill has no healing properties, but when the doctor tells us that this is the magic pill that will cure us, we put our faith in the doctor, and we are healed. What about invasive surgeries? The placebo effect is successfully applied to sham knee surgeries. The doctor goes to great lengths to create the illusion of a surgery. The patient is anesthetized, and an incision is made. A video of the procedure is shown on a monitor, and the conversation during the procedure corresponds with the video. The tray of instruments is displayed. This has been done for many knee surgeries, and the sham surgery is as effective as the actual surgery. The results have been documented in many medical journals. I saw one man interviewed who had had the sham knee surgery. With tears of gratitude, he told of how he can now play basketball and dance, things he was unable to do before the surgery. When doctors are aware of the success of the placebo effect, why are they in disbelief when they see a spontaneous remission? This is energy healing, and we need to know more about this energy.

I have experienced my own "miracle healing." I woke up one morning, and a large area of the vision in my right eye was blocked. I was diagnosed with a retinal venial occlusion. The doctor could not unblock the vein, and it was hopeless and incurable. For eight years, the doctor kept a close watch and tried to contain the damage. He gave me a shot in my eye periodically. Ouch! At every visit, the doctor would take a scan of my eye. The image was over 50 percent red where the blockage was. The vein showed a puffy, bubbly surface on top.

In order to heal, I first needed to find the original cause for the vein shutting down. Looking back at my life, I saw that there were things happening at the time my vision changed that I didn't want to look at. Our subconscious mind is literal. A beloved family member was destroying themselves with addictions, and there were three small children at risk.

This was difficult to watch. In the eight years that my vision had been compromised, the situation had improved, but I still needed to be at peace with the original cause. When we experience trauma, it is always with us until we can release it. After coming to peace, I needed to believe that my vision was perfect spiritually and mentally. When I was able to make these changes in my subconscious mind, I was able to attract a facilitator for self-healing into my life. As he brought the energy into my body, my body intelligence knew what to do with these frequencies in order to heal itself.

The block was gone, and I could see perfectly. At my next doctor's visit, my eye tested 20/20. Where there had been red on the scan, it was now blue, and the vein was smooth. I was jumping for joy, and I thought that the doctor would be happy for me. He was nonreactive but did ask what I had done. I told him I used energy healing. He pretended that nothing had changed. His response was, "Well, I guess that it's not doing any harm." The medical world doesn't understand energy healing and is more comfortable ignoring it altogether. The nobel Prize winning physicist Brian Joseph calls this "Pathological Disbelief', a condition he describes as" I wouldn't believe it even if it were true". And my doctors last words to me were, "I don't think you need an injection today."

Researching, I can't find that this condition has ever been healed before. I feel like Roger Bannister, who was the first man to run the mile in less than four minutes. It was thought that running the mile in under four minutes was unachievable and possibly fatal for anyone who tried. Roger created a new belief of what was achievable in track. Now people know that it is possible to do something that was considered impossible, and more people are able to run the mile in less than four minutes. As people's beliefs change, a new reality is formed.

As Henry Ford told us when we make an assumption that something is impossible to do, it is impossible. When we remove all the limitations and believe that is it possible to do, it is possible. We now know that what was considered impossible is now possible and a new reality is created. My eye condition was considered hopeless and incurable and now we know that it can be cured.

Matter is an illusion, and there are endless possibilities in outcomes when we consider quantum physics and the power of God. How are you using this invisible power? You have the choice of where you focus your power.

Have you ever thought of aging as an illness? All our lives, we have watched everyone age. People lose their mobility, and their minds get forgetful or worse. This has always been our role model. With every symptom that is related to aging, we are reminded that it is happening to us. We believe that we need to get sick and have a painful and expensive end-of-life experience. What if we could make a shift in our perception about aging? We will age chronologically, but our bodies and minds can stay young. Using different modalities, we can reverse the aging process. This begins with a change in our beliefs. I am going through the process now. It is so exciting to experience this transformation. If I can do it, you can do it to. Begin by knowing that you can stay young at any age. Remember the crazy way quantum physics works, and know that all things are possible.

THE HUMAN GENOME PROJECT

The idea of the Human Genome Project began in 1984. The basic premise was that the genes we are born with determine our lives. The study was established to prove that we inherit disease, illness, addictions, and character traits from our parents. We are victims of our genes. It was and still is the world's largest collaborative biological project. England, Japan, China, Australia, Saudi Arabia, United States, Estonia, France, United Arab Emirates, and Turkey all participated. It was launched in 1990 with the United States funding three billion dollars (in 1990s valuations). The project was completed thirteen years later in 2003. Today, seventeen years after this study has been completed, the results are still "in their initial stages. "Initial stages" means that there is no proof that our genes determine our destiny. This multibillion-dollar worldwide study could show *no evidence* that our genes have much influence on our lives.

Another eighteen million dollars has been spent on deciding the legal and ethical questions that have been raised by the study. One of the ethical questions raised was the fear that employers or insurance companies would refuse to hire or insure individuals because of health concerns indicated by someone's genes.

IT'S THE ENVIRONMENT

Dr. Bruce Lipton is a cell biologist, author and internationally recognized leader in bridging the gap between science and Spirit.

He was teaching at Wisconsin's School of Medicine. His life was in shambles and he decided to move to the Caribbean. He wanted to be away from academia and its rigid structure.

In his laboratory in the fall of 1985, he had an epiphany. He cloned a single cell until he had thousands of replications of one cell. They were all genetically identical. He placed them in different mediums. They became the medium that he put them in. One became fat, one became muscle, and one became bone.

The determining factor of the cell was not the genes but the physical and energetic environment that surrounded the cell.

He revealed that the environment operating through the membrane controlled the behavior and physiology of the cell, turning the genes off and on. Here were molecular pathways that connect the mind to the body. The new discovery went against the accepted theory of mainstream medicine and Dr. Lipton's findings were slow to be recognized. We now acknowledge a new science called epigenetics as even today the medical field continues to rely heavily on genetic determinism.

By applying this knowledge Dr. Lipton transformed his life. With the awareness that our mind is controlling our lives he realized that we are not just our bodies but spiritual beings. Here was the bridge that connected science and spirituality. When he applied the new brain science to his life his physical and mental well being improved. Dr. Lipton knew the powerful ramifications this had on the lives of all human beings. Of course, we are more complicated than a single cell in a Petri dish. Our bodies are made up of approximately fifty trillion single cells.

In our bodies, our cells are being impacted by our hormones. Our perceptions and beliefs are determining whether something is scary or safe. Our minds are signaling to the nervous system which hormones to secrete into our bodies. These hormones are determining the environment that our cells are living in.

When you decide that something is stressful or scary, you secrete stress hormones into your body: adrenaline, cortisol, and norepinephrine. All stress is internally generated by one's attitudes. It is not life's events, but one's reaction to them, that activates the stress hormone response. When these hormones are released into your system, the growth and repair functions are shut down. Your immune system is compromised, your digestive system shuts down, and you pack fat on your body; your brain becomes foggy.

When we were running from a hungry wild animal, it served us well that our bodily functions shut down, so we could use all our energy to move fast and get out of danger. When we were safe, we could turn off the stress response and relax in our cave on a comfy rock with some fresh-picked berries. What did we do to relax?

In our modern society, we operate in stress most of the day; we are overscheduled, rushed, in debt, fighting with our teenager, getting a scary diagnosis. Fill in the blanks. The problem is that the stress hormones are not serving us now. When we experience stress in our bodies often and over long periods of time, we create illness and disease. What we think is killing us.

When you decide that something is safe and fun, you secrete the bliss hormones into your body: oxytocin and anandamide. These regulate and keep the body in a state of balance. These hormones boost your immune and repair system and clear your mind. You are able to digest and assimilate your food, so that you are not putting fat on your body. By consistently secreting the bliss hormone, you ensure yourself of a long, happy, healthy life.

We have some wonderful examples of people living long happy lives due to their ability to consistently release the bliss hormone.

My husband, Bob, and I saw George Burns in Chasens's Restaurant in Beverly Hills. This is where the Hollywood elite used to hang out back in the day (closed 1995). Mr. Burns was sitting at the bar, drinking his liquor, smoking his cigar, and surrounded by ladies. He was well into his nineties at the time. At the age of ninety-six, he signed a lifetime contract with Caesars' Palace in Las Vegas. He lived to be a hundred and was entertaining until the end.

Betty White is another example. At this printing, she is ninety-eight. Her career has spanned eighty years. In 2017, she was celebrated as the First Lady of Television. She is the oldest person to host *Saturday Night Live.*

Quotes from Ms. White:

"I eat hot dogs, and I drink vodka."

"I am actually the happiest old broad alive. Half my life is working in a profession that I love, and the other half is working with animals."

She was married to the love of her life: Allen Ludden. She is still in demand in her career and works tirelessly to care for animals.

These icons have had amazing careers and have had great love in their lives. They have dedicated their lives to bringing laughter into other people's lives. It's true, laughter is the best medicine. Their long, healthy lives have not depended upon a healthy lifestyle, although I recommend that as well. Think about the hormones that have been pumping in their bodies.

Another example can be seen in the lives of great musicians, composers, and conductors. How frequently they continue productive careers into their eighties and nineties. Their lives have been dedicated to the creation and embodiment of beauty.

I had a friend named Mary Lou who lived to age ninety-six and was another example. She took a personal interest in everyone. There were always parties in her home on the beach in Malibu. If you went to any crowded restaurant in Malibu without reservations, if you were with Mary Lou, you got seated right away. She was known and loved by everyone. She traveled the world and invited people to come to her home, and they did. You could drop by anytime and meet interesting people from around the world. She had lost the key and never locked the door. When you entered, there was always a gathering in her large living room or out on the deck. There might be a party going on. I attended her eightieth birthday party. Mary Lou had made a mockup of the Pearly Gates. She came down the staircase and through the Pearly Gates in a flowing gown. I asked a man I was chatting with how he knew Mary Lou. He said, "I'm the TV repairman. I came last week to fix her television, and she invited me to the party." Mary Lou had lived on that beach since the 1950s, and she had hob knobbed with many celebrities. She drank with Flip Wilson. She knew Lee Marvin, Shirley MacLaine, John Travolta, and many others. She told a story of the time when Sir Lawrence Olivier was living next door to her. She was throwing a party, and she needed to borrow something, as neighbors often do. She went next door and asked, "Larry, I'm throwing a party and I need to borrow something. Can I borrow your valet?" Well, of course, he couldn't say no; after all, it was Mary Lou.

I showed up one day and stayed later than I had planned. The group decided to take a walk on the beach. I hadn't brought a sweatshirt, and it gets quite cold on the beach after sundown. Mary Lou trotted off to her room to get me something to wear. Out she came with a full-length mink coat. My mouth dropped as I said, "I can't wear that. We'll be walking in the sand." She put the coat on me and pushed me out the door. I walked on the beach in Malibu in a full-length mink coat. I felt like a diva, like Joan Crawford in the opening scene of *Mildred Pierce*. But that was Mary Lou; whatever she had was to be shared. By the way this coat had been bought long before PETA discovered how they sourced mink fur.

Mary Lou lived in her home until her death. She often had a Pepperdine College student there to help out and be her companion. There were parties until the end of her life. The party that her children gave her as a celebration of life was amazing. There was valet parking and a catered full bar and meal service. It lasted a full day and into the night, and hundreds of people attended. She got the great send off that she deserved. She had had a great love in her life and was deeply loved by her children and grandchildren.

I'm very grateful that I got to know and experience Mary Lou. I learned many lessons. She welcomed and engaged with everyone. When she spoke to you, you knew she was genuinely interested in you, your family, and your life. She made you feel like you were truly being listened to and being heard. She ate whatever she wanted and had a glass of champagne almost every night. She is another example of someone living a long and full life because of the bliss hormones pumping through her body.

THE CHANGE PROCESS

In order to change your life you need to make changes in the beliefs that are in your subconscious mind. This is below consciousness, so how do we access this part of the mind? Are you familiar with kinesiology? Muscle testing? You may have had a positive or negative experience using kinesiology. There are many ways to use muscle testing and many different things that you can muscle test for. Many years ago I went to a Chiropractor who muscle tested me for supplements using a pendulum. Clinical research on the physiology of the nervous system and the holistic functioning of the body resulted in the development of kinesiology in the 1970s. Kinesiology exposed for the first time the intimate connection between mind and body, revealing that the mind thinks with the body itself. It provided a way to discover what the mind was thinking by using muscles in the body.

Although the term "muscle testing" is used, what we really are testing is the energy flow in the body. Deepak Chopra puts it this way: "Every cell in your body is eavesdropping on what your mind is thinking." It is the wormhole between two universes—the physical world and the world of the mind and spirit—an interface between dimensions. Here is a tool to recover and demonstrate for all to see, the lost connection with the higher reality. This is demonstrated by the fact that when you are thinking about something you like, you will muscle test strong. When you are thinking about something you don't like, you will muscle test weak. When you are telling the truth, your muscles will test strong. When you are telling a lie, your muscles will test weak. The moment you have the thought, your emotions and your truth are communicated, and your body responds.

In the addendum of Dr. Bruce Lipton's groundbreaking book, *The Biology of Belief,* he spoke of a change modality called PSYCH-K®. This mind-change modality uses kinesiology to demonstrate what is going on in your subconscious mind. PSYCH-K® is a way to change the beliefs that are in your subconscious mind and thus change your life. Dr. Lipton is confident of its integrity, simplicity, and effectiveness.

I have mentioned the mind and will discuss it more fully later. Not to confuse the mind with the brain, the mind is the non physical part of your thinking process.

So now let's look at the brain the physical organ inside your skull. You have a left hemisphere that controls the right side of your body. It is responsible for logical thought and reason, thinks in words, deals in specifics, analyses, thinks sequentially, identifies with the individual, compartmentalizes and puts things in order. The right hemisphere controls the left side of the body. It is responsible for emotions, intuition, creativity, thinks in pictures, deals in wholes, will put things together, thinks simultaneously, identifies with groups, and is spontaneous. These are separated by the corpus callosum.

As we go through our day we may be using the left side of our brain to balance our checkbook and then the right side of our brain to paint a painting. This is brain dominance of one side or the other. When both sides are engaged we are in a whole brain state. This is the time of super learning and we have the ability to make changes. Using PSYCH-K® we can go into a whole brain posture and create a whole brain state that will facilitate change in your subconscious mind.

I discovered research by a neuroscientist, Jeffrey L. Fannin, PhD, who is an expert in brain mapping. His brain mapping showed that a PSYCH-K® balance produced changes in the brain. There was objective and radical change in EG activity, leading to a balanced brainwave energy pattern also referred to as the whole brain state. This is a state of coherency in the brain marked by a bilateral, symmetrical brainwave pattern that allows for maximum communication and data flow between the left and the right hemisphere of the brain. Dr. Fannin reports that the PSYCH-K® belief-modification process enhances our functioning by optimizing belief systems and brain function.

The PSYCH-K® process was downloaded to Rob Williams in 1985. He was able to transcribe and teach this amazing work. These are simple, empowering techniques that change the beliefs and perceptions in your subconscious mind. The impact is that you make changes at a cellular level. The secret of life is your beliefs rather than your genes.

I use PSYCH-K®, and it has completely changed my life. I had lost Bob, the love of my life, whom I had been with for thirty-one years. I was filled with fears. Would I have enough money? Who would take care of me if I got sick? Who was I now that

I was alone? I felt very vulnerable and alone. I had an addicted daughter who had finally gotten sober. How do I deal with her? I wasn't sleeping. I was drinking too much and too often. I was an artist who wasn't painting. I was low in energy and probably depressed. It was like living half a life and I didn't know it.

Using PSYCH-K®, I began to heal myself. I was able to bring all the traumas around the deaths I had experienced in my childhood to peace. I began to treasure the great love I had experienced with Bob and realize what a great gift I had been given. I was able to discover and release limiting beliefs and low self-esteem that I harbored. After using PSYCH-K® I was able to see myself as having clarity, courage, inner strength, detachment from past traumas, confidence, peace, calm, and connection with others. I have been able to help others help themselves. I have a deeper sense of peace and satisfaction mentally, emotionally, physically, and spiritually.

I am sleeping and traveling. I am inspired and creative. I am filled with energy, and I seldom drink. My mental clarity is too important to me. I found the inspiration to write this book. New opportunities are showing up, and people with knowledge and skills are collaborating with me. My income is increasing.

Joan

I became a PSYCH-K® facilitator. Shortly after my basic PSYCH-K® workshop, I went on a retreat to Lake Arrowhead with my spiritual center. My friend Joan accompanied me. Joan had been brutally attacked just three weeks before the retreat. She thought she was going to be killed. This had been a terrifying experience for her. She came to the retreat with cuts and bruises on her face. As we sat together one afternoon, I asked if she would like to bring this terrifying experience to peace and nonattachment. She said yes. We spent a few minutes in a PSYCH-K® balance, and she indicated that the process was complete. Then she told me that she had a fear of public speaking and asked me if I could help her with that. We did another balance to release her fear of public speaking.

After dinner we went into a large room where we knew they were going to pass the microphone around for anybody who wanted to speak. Joan said, "I'm going, but I'm not going to speak." The meeting began, and Joan was the fourth one to grab the microphone. She stood up in front of a hundred people and told her story of being attacked. She told the story without crying and even without emotion!

When the meeting was over, I asked her if she realized what she had done. Her response was, "I think I could have told the story better." Her fear was gone, and her behavior had changed, but her conscious mind was unaware that changes had been made.

The story of the attack was an important story for us to hear. She needed our love and support.

Lea

Lea's family struggled for money. She wore homemade clothes and hand-me-downs. When she was sick, there was no money for a doctor. She had very low self-esteem, and she got good at blending in. She became a caretaker of everyone else, often at the expense of her own needs. She attracted people and situations that reinforced her belief about herself.

She had married two men who were emotionally unavailable. In the first marriage, there was a major lack of communication. The second marriage was to a man who was emotionally shut down. She joined the military. It was a man's world, and she felt she was given the job because the military needed to fill a quota to hire women. Her bosses were domineering and thought a woman's place in the service was to be a secretary, clerk, or nurse. She felt that she didn't matter. She completed college (a first in her family) and got her master's degree, working hard in order to get promoted. She was deployed and bravely served, attaining the rank of colonel. Seeing her accomplishments through the lens of her low self-esteem, she didn't give herself credit for her successes.

After using PSYCH-K, Lea became aware of her lack of self-worth and limiting beliefs. She learned to love and respect herself and to finally find true happiness within herself.

She found the courage to speak out for herself. She left her controlling husband and retired from the military. Now she is off her medication and traveling the world, fulfilling her dream.

Clara

Clara grew up doing without extras. There were six children in the family, and her mother was a stay-at-home wife. Money was very tight. When Clara was seven, her mother got very sick and, was taken to the hospital. She was there for three months. During this time, Clara's father fed the family fast food and rewarded them with candy. When Clara's mother returned, she was shocked at how fat her children had become.

Fast food and candy were what Clara used to comfort herself. It had been terrifying to have her mother disappear and to not know if or when she would return. Using food as a coping mechanism created major weight gain. For the next fifty years, Clara struggled with weight management. She ballooned up to three hundred pounds at one time. She tried every-weight loss modality— Overeaters Anonymous, liquid diets, fasting, even surgery. As she struggled over and over again with not losing the weight or losing it with great effort and then gaining it back, she was given the message that she must be doing something wrong. She needed more willpower. She felt like a failure. A well-meaning colleague told her that her weight was holding her back in her career.

Clara was accomplished in many areas of her life. She was smart and hard working. She worked her way through college and held a responsible job. She attracted a loving and devoted husband who loved Clara for who she was and at any weight.

Clara was miserable carrying the extra weight. She saw the way people looked at her and judged her. It was hard for her to be social. Finding something to wear was a nightmare. She didn't fit into chairs, and she judged herself the most harshly.

After discovering PSYCH-K®, she was finally able to attain and maintain her ideal weight. She was able to release the old traumas around being without her mother. She was able to change her beliefs about food. It was never about willpower; it was about hidden beliefs in her subconscious mind. Once those beliefs were uncovered and replaced with beliefs of loving herself and knowing she was meant to be in a healthy body, she was able to lose the weight without effort. She wakes up each day without the obsessive thoughts of, what will I eat today? Will I fail again? Now she is feeling confident about who she is. She loves shopping for clothes, and she dresses stylishly. She is earning promotions in her career.

YOUR MIND

The mind is the part of you that enables you to think, feel emotions and be aware of things. You mind is invisible and transcendent. This is the world of thought, feelings, attitudes, beliefs and imagination. The purpose of the mind is to absorb information, transform it into knowledge and lead us to action. The mind is about mental processing, thought and consciousness. There are 3 parts of mind: The conscious mind, the subconscious mind and the superconscious mind. We need to understand their purpose and how they work.

THE CONSCIOUS MIND

The conscious mind is the part of the mind that follows our direction. It's like the tip of the iceberg, the part we are aware of. We only use it 5% of the day.

We are the one behind the mind telling it what to think about. We can squander our mind by letting it run freely, we can use it destructively or constructively.

Squander, stream of thought:

Look at that blue sky. That's the color blue of my favorite dress when I was 7 years old. Jack got mud on that dress the first time I wore it. I never forgave him. I think he's a doctor now. Oh Yeah, I need to make an appointment with my doctor for a check up

You can see how the mind wanders. Have you ever listened to people who talk like this?

Destructively

We can use our conscious mind to attract negative events into our lives. We think about uncomfortable situations either past or future, our problems, our worries. We can gossip and criticize. We can spend time dwelling on the unfairness of the world. We can obsess, turning it over and over again in our mind. These thoughts are churning us up inside and releasing toxic stress hormones into our body and making us sick. They are also the thoughts that manifest unwanted events in our life.

Constructively

We can use our conscious mind for new creations, learning new skills and gaining new information. We can paint, write, figure out a strategy or a solution to a problem. We can use our imagination to bring our desires into our reality.

You are not your mind. You are the one who is choosing what you want to focus on. Your true essence, your life force is the one who is directing your conscious mind.

I'm not saying that you must always be using your mind for improvement. There are times when we choose to watch a silly movie or read a good mystery and let our mind be frivolous. But I am suggesting that you be aware of how you are using your mind and know that you can divert your mind to choose a different experience.

The conscious mind is the part of the mind that we are aware of. We set goals, and we judge our results. We compare and contrast. This part of the mind is time bound. We put events on our calendar and make sure we arrive on time. We can recall experiences from the past, and we can visualize into the future. In this part of our minds, we have very limited processing capacity. Our short-term memory is approximately twenty seconds long. We process an average of forty bits of information per second. We can retain only one to three events at a time.

With the conscious mind, we read books, attend lectures, and gather information. It is the seat of our knowledge. But gaining knowledge does not change our behavior.

THE SUBCONSCIOUS MIND

Your subconscious mind was formed during your childhood. This is the part of the iceberg that is below the water line. It is in charge 95% of the time. Remember it is not your genes that are determining your life, but your beliefs. Here is where your beliefs are buried. When you can change your beliefs of low self esteem to beliefs of confidence you will make sustainable changes in your life. When you can let go of fear, pain, suffering, stress and anxiety you can instantly replace them with confidence, peace, joy and ease.

From birth to age seven, we are operating in a theta brainwave state. This means we are recording everything we see and hear. We are absorbing and copying everything in our environment. We are created this way so we can become independent human beings as quickly as possible. This is our subconscious programming, and what we are learning in those early years become our coping skills for the rest of our lives. The Jesuits have known this for over four hundred years. They have said, "Give me a child until the age of seven, and I will show you the man." We are downloading programs from our environment: our parents, siblings, teachers, and peers. We are not choosing, editing, or filtering. We are accepting everything that is presented to us as truth. Somewhere around the age of eight, we begin operating on beta brainwaves, where we can discern and make judgments, but we still need others' input for our protection.

When we become adults and have the ability to make sensible decisions for ourselves, we still look to others for instructions. Our education and community values are based on rules, compliance, and rewards for obedience. We are conditioned to look to others for guidance and find "experts" to tell us what to do. Outside elements are making our decisions and we do not feel responsible for what is happening in our lives. Our boss can fire us and has the power to promote us. The mortgage company determines if we get the loan. The school determines what our children learn. Social norms determine our family structure. With so many outside influences, it's not surprising that we don't feel in charge of our own lives. We do not see ourselves as our own source of power and authority. We have abdicated our power to outside forces. We have lost confidence in our ability to make our own decisions. When we don't feel in control of our own lives, it follows we also take no accountability for the decisions that we make. We feel limited by rules, expectations and demands. Because we feel trapped, we may have emotions of anger, resentment, or blame. We may have unknowingly embraced the belief that we have no personal power, free will, or sovereignty.

We yield to the authority of society, family, and other pressures because we feel that we require something from these sources. We need approval, acceptance, protection and love. We feel that these supports may be withdrawn if we go rogue and actually begin to think for ourselves. We are taught that we may be unworthy or undeserving of love and acceptance if we step outside family and social norms.

When we become aware that we are more than our conscious mind and connect to our subconscious and superconscious mind, we begin to listen to our inner voice, which beckons us to remember who we are. We are, in fact, highly evolved beings who can never truly lose our truth but can possibly forget it for a time. We begin to remember that we have personal power, free will, and sovereignty. We have the power to make all the right and sometimes not-so-right decisions. And we learn.

In this awakened state of mind, where we begin to practice free will and personal sovereignty, we have a deep inner knowing that guides us to embrace a further truth. We realize that we no longer need the structure and rules of our social climate. We break free of cultural expectations and we begin to trust ourselves. We each have our own voice, moral compass, right action, peace, and calm. We are free of the lie that we require an outside source to provide us with what we need. We have all we need inside us.

You are your greatest resource when you take back your power. No one has the power to make you truly happy or sad. You are in charge of everything having to do with you. This is the most empowering mind-set anyone could ever have.

The subconscious mind is the warehouse of all our beliefs, and it also monitors the operation of the body—motor functions, heart rate, digestion. It thinks literally. Whatever you plant is what will grow. The subconscious is always focused on the present moment. In the subconscious mind, we have expanded processing capacity. Our memory can recall past experiences, attitudes, values, and beliefs. Here we can recall thousands of events at a time. Our processing capacity averages forty million bits of information per second. What we have recorded in the subconscious is always playing in the background. We operate from our subconscious mind 95 percent of the time.

As you can see, this is where the power of the mind resides. We can gather information in the conscious mind; we can memorize a book and become inspired by a workshop, but nothing in our lives change. Will power and positive thinking doesn't work. I've tried it, and I imagine you've tried it too. How has it worked for you? It is in the subconscious mind where lasting changes happen. In the subconscious, we can change our beliefs and our perspectives. It is then that our lives change. All things are possible.

THE SUPERCONSCIOUS MIND

This is the part of the mind that sees the bigger picture of your life. This is a level of awareness that is beyond material reality and taps into the energy and consciousness of God. The superconscious mind is the essence of the universe – a flow of electromagnetic waves that permeate all matter and space. In the change process, we will always check in with this part of the mind to ensure that our goals are both safe and appropriate in the context of our lives. This part of the mind is nonlinear and timeless. It processes with unlimited speed and capacity. This is Spirit or our life force.

YOU ARE RESPONSIBLE FOR EVERYTHING IN YOUR LIFE

With this paradigm shift, you are now face to face with the realization that you are responsible for everything you've experienced in your life. Let me explain.

Once we realize that we have been using cosmic energy to mold our life we must accept responsibility for everything that is in our life. Take credit for the beauty, love, abundance and health in your life. Take responsibility for the ugly, fear, lack and decease in your life.

It may be painful and scary to take responsibility. Taking the position "It's not my fault" is destructive. When you are looking outside yourself to see who's to blame for your predicament you are engaging in toxic justification. You feel that the world is doing catastrophic things to you and there is nothing you can do to change the situation. There is always someone to blame and it may make you feel righteous for awhile but you are not getting to the cause and you will continue to be the helpless victim. You will repeat the same mistakes.

When you realize that you are the master of your domain and you are in control of your life you step into your power. You become the victor. This is freeing. If you have created a mess you now know that you have the ability to clean it up. Your power resides in your ability to make this paradigm shift. You can create any good thing that you can imagine.

Everything is first a thought before it manifests in form. You are using the power to create all the time whether you are aware of it or not. You have thoughts in your subconscious mind that you are unaware of yet you are manifesting these thoughts into your life. So let's dissect the process and see how our subconscious mind creates situations without our conscious knowledge.

When you look back at your childhood, you can see that you've recreated some of it, and it is in your life today. Your alcoholic father may show up as an abusive husband. Your overbearing mother may show up as a controlling wife. Notice the patterns in your life: repeated bad relationships, financial losses, health challenges. You did not deliberately create this, but it was familiar, and as those recorded tapes continue to play, you are drawn to the familiar.

Now, of course you say, "I didn't want this accident or illness. That wasn't a familiar experience in my childhood."

In this universe, where everything is connected with everything else, there is no such thing as an accident. A sudden and unexpected accident may appear to be random, unrelated to observable causes, but the actual origin can be traced through research. Even accident proneness involves numerous small preparatory steps before the so-called accident occurs. Remember the chaos theory; there are unsuspected connections that actually have an inner hidden relationship.

A sudden illness has been created by thought patterns. A disease in the body is evidence that there are subconscious beliefs supporting the development of the disease. Treating the disease on a physical level does not address the cause. We must treat the cause by becoming aware of the messages we have taken into our subconscious mind that are inviting the illness into our body. Whatever beliefs we hold have consequences, for better or worse. Our thoughts caused the illness, and by changing our thoughts, we can release the illness. This is why no condition is incurable or hopeless. The doctors told me that my vision would never improve; incurable and hopeless, and yet my eye is healed.

Let me give you a case study of how cancer gets into your body, and I'll use myself as an example.

When I was four, my mother died of cancer, and later my father did too. We were taken in by my paternal grandparents. My grandmother died of cancer when I was ten. Many of my aunts, uncles, and great aunts died of cancer. As I was growing up, I was told that I had the "cancer gene." As a teen, I walked to the beach with my transistor radio and sunbathed with my friends. I was a redhead. I freckled and burned. I later learned that exposure to the sun caused cancer. Whenever I go to the doctor's office, I fill out an intake form. The question that is always asked is, "What diseases did your mother, father, grandparents, and siblings have?" And there I am writing the word *cancer* over and over again. I turn on the TV, and there is a commercial telling me where to get the best cancer treatment. I have watched as my sister and many of my friends have had cancer diagnoses. My beloved husband died of cancer. These are messages that are being taken into my subconscious mind.

Last year, I got a cancer diagnosis. Can you guess which organ was affected? It showed up as skin cancer. Our skin is the largest organ in the body. The purpose of skin is protection. How protected did I feel during my childhood? The people I loved and trusted to take care of me kept dying. During my childhood, I never felt protected. Bob, who was my protector, died and left me unprotected. And where on my skin did the cancer show up? My left middle finger. The finger we use to flip someone off. Ha! According to Louise Hay, that finger stands for anger and sexuality. I was probably pretty angry about losing so many people I loved. And I have always been concerned about my libido. I worried if I was normal. I love

Lily Tomlin's definition of normal: "Normal is a setting on the washing machine."

This explains how disease comes into our body. It isn't that we consciously invite the disease in, but the subliminal messages bring it to us.

Having the cancer cut out removed the symptom, but it did not address the cause. Even after the cancer is gone, the doctor will always remind you that it can come back, another powerful message that produces expectations of more cancer in your body.

Remember, it began with the beliefs that were embedded in my subconscious mind. To treat the cause, I needed to identify the messages I had taken into my subconscious mind that caused me to believe I was destined to get cancer, and I needed to install new beliefs that would support my health.

Cancer-Causing Beliefs

- I've inherited the cancer gene.
- As we age, most people get cancer.
- Almost everyone in my family has had cancer.
- I have exposed myself to cancer-causing sun rays.

Health-Enhancing Beliefs

- Cancer is not carried in the genes.

- I experience a harmonious balance of mind, body, and spirit.
- I choose to live a vibrant and healthy life.
- My body is cancer free.

NOBODY CAN CURE YOU

Let me be clear—nobody can change your circumstances or heal your illness. The processes I am talking about are designed to identify and resolve beliefs that are stressful or are in conflict with what you want. Using these processes, you can release the beliefs that are impacting you negatively and incorporate the new beliefs that support your healing and allow changes of circumstances to create what you desire.

The power to change is within you. Healing is a result of personal restoration of spiritual, emotional, and physical balance.

When we are going through difficult times, we often feel that we have limited choices or that we need to be rescued. If instead we can change that perception so that we can see ourselves as limitless and powerful, we can release our limitations and recognize our infinite potential.

Your goal is to discover and change those subconscious beliefs and programming that are negatively impacting your life and replace them with positive beliefs. When this transformation is accomplished, exciting and profound results often occur. It is impossible to predict what will change for you. The practical result is significantly more capacity and potential to manifest your desired outcome.

The universe is waiting anxiously as we choose, instant by instant, which path to follow. Every act, thought, and choice adds to the permanent tapestry; our decisions ripple through the universe to affect all life. This is not theoretical. Everything is connected to everything else. What once may have been thought of as metaphysical is now based on fact and confirmed by science.

CHAPTER 5

GOD AND SCIENCE

For a long time, our perception has been that God and science were in disagreement. That has never been true. It is the Church, not God, which decreed that science was making claims that were against God. The church denounced Copernicus's writings six decades after their publication. The Church rejected the theory that the Earth revolved around the sun. Giordano Bruno was burned at the stake by the Inquisition for declaring that the earth was round and that there were other solar systems. The great debate of creationism of the Bible and evolutionism of Darwin went on for years. These battles were instigated by the church against science. There is nothing that God is against. Science has traditionally recognized religion as "airy fairy" and unsubstanciated. A truce was declared. There was an agreement that science would be concerned with the natural world and religion would be concerned with the supernatural world. They would explore separate domains. And now with advanced technology we discover that they both work the same way.

How are God and science the same?

They both use cosmic energy.

We can't see the energy, but we see its effects.

This power works in mysterious ways; anything is possible.

They prove connection and interaction with everything.

They demonstrate order in the world.

This power is for you to use.

GOD IS SO MUCH MORE THAN SCIENCE

The attributes of God are light, love, truth, compassion, joy, kindness, integrity, justice, and goodness. There are core principles and spiritual truths.

God gifts us with downloads, epiphanies, guidance, grace, and once in a while, for the more enlightened, that feeling of ecstasy that comes with seeing God.

The lost connection with our higher reality has been reestablished. We can interface with the two dimensions of the physical world and the world of mind and spirit.

Kinesiology now allows a window into all the hidden programs that are running our lives. We can access them and change them. We are no longer prisoners of the limiting beliefs that others have downloaded into our subconscious mind without our knowledge or permission. By using PSYCH-K®, we can change these beliefs to positive, life-supporting beliefs, and we are awakened to our personal power. We can dissolve phobias that have been with us our entire life and bring traumatic experiences to peace and non attachment. We can attract success and abundance, overcome bad habits, and bring loving relationships into our lives. As our behavior is changed on a subconscious level, we can stop trying to control ourselves on a conscious level by using willpower and positive thinking and stop blaming ourselves. In this awakened state of mind, we each have our own voice, moral compass, right action, peace, and calm.

You have everything you need inside you. No one has the power to make you happy or sad. You are in charge of everything that has to do with you. You are a highly evolved individual, and what you are thinking impacts your life and the destiny of the world. Everything is connected, and you are making a difference.

When we lift our own vibration, we impact the entire world. Our thoughts and actions are rippling out into the universe. When we change, the world changes.

"Be the change you wish to see in the world."—Gandhi

"In a gentle way you can shake the world." —Gandhi

God and science are in agreement. Their power is transmitted through electromagnetic energy. We are becoming aware of this power that permeates each of us and the entire universe. We are one with All that is. We increase our power by increasing our integrity, understanding and compassion. We are living in a time when we can accelerate our human potential beyond anything we have ever imagined.

My desire is to continue to awaken and evolve spiritually and to uplift the world. Please join me.

BIBLIOGRAPHY

Hawkins, M.D., Ph.D. David R, Power vs. Force, Carlsbad, CA Hay House, 1998 Hay House

Hay, Louise, You Can Heal Your Life, Carlsbd, CA Hay House, 2004

Hicks, Ester and Jerry, The Amazing Power of Deliberate Intent, Carlsbad, CA, Hay House, 2006

Lipton, Ph.D. Bruce H., The Biiology of Belief, Carlsbad, CA, Hay House, 2015

Wattles, Wallace D., The Science of Getting Rich, Blacksburg, VA, Thrifty Books, 2009

Other Sources

PSYCH-K®International.com

MindMovies.com

FineArtByLinda; my art website

ABOUT THE AUTHOR

Linda Gauthier was born and raised in Santa Monica, California. She was orphaned at the age of four and raised by three sets of parents. With all the death she experienced, she became a spiritual seeker at a very young age, asking, "Why am I here?" and "Where do people go when they die?"

She has built her own insurance agency and traveled the world She is a licensed private pilot, an artist, and an author. Linda is a Science of Mind Practitioner and a PSYCH-K® facilitator.

She has two wonderful daughters and six amazing grandchildren.

When Linda discovered and experienced a way for people to let go of fear, pain, suffering, stress and anxiety and embrace confidence, peace, joy and freedom she was excited to share the process.

Linda is committed to her own spiritual evolution and the upliftment of all mankind.

Powerful + important
My body is complete
just the way it is

The photo on the cover is a sunset
taken from Linda's balcony.

Sunsets are God's way of showing us
that endings can be beautiful.
—Beau Tapin

9 781982 255107